The Shakespeare Library

The Merchant of Venice

WENDY GREENHILL

HEAD OF EDUCATION
ROYAL SHAKESPEARE COMPANY

and

PAUL WIGNALL

Heinemann
LIBRARY

First published in Great Britain by Heinemann Library
Halley Court, Jordan Hill, Oxford OX2 8EJ
a division of Reed Educational & Professional Publishing Ltd

OXFORD   FLORENCE   PRAGUE   MADRID   ATHENS
MELBOURNE   AUCKLAND   KUALA LUMPUR   SINGAPORE   TOKYO
IBADAN   NAIROBI   KAMPALA   JOHANNESBURG   GABORONE
PORTSMOUTH NH (USA)   CHICAGO   MEXICO CITY   SAO PAULO

Designed by Ken Vail Graphic Design, Cambridge
Printed in Great Britain by Bath Press Colourbooks, Glasgow

01 00 99 98 97
10 9 8 7 6 5 4 3 2 1

ISBN 0 431 07536 0

British Library Cataloguing in Publication Data

Greenhill, Wendy
The Merchant of Venice – (The Shakespeare library)
1. Shakespeare, William, 1564-1616. Merchant of Venice – Juvenile literature
2. English drama – Early Modern and Elizabethan, 1500–1600
– History and criticism – Juvenile literature
I.Title II.Wignall, Paul
822.3'3

Acknowledgements
The authors and publishers would like to thank the following for permission
to reproduce photographs and other illustrative material:

The British Library, pages 14, 22;
The British Museum, page 5;
The National Portrait Gallery, page 4;
Donald Cooper: Photostage, pages 11, 13, 15, 20, 28, 29, 31;
The Shakespeare Centre Library: Stratford-upon-Avon,
cover & pages 6, 7, 8, 9, 10 ,16, 19, 21, 23 ,24 (right), 27 (both), 30;
The Victoria and Albert Museum, pages 18, 24 (left).

Our thanks to Jean Black for her comments in the preparation of this book.

In preparing this book, the authors have used the text of *The Merchant of Venice* from
William Shakespeare The Complete Works, Clarendon Press, Oxford 1986.

Names in **bold** in the text are characters in the play.

CONTENTS

INTRODUCTION

By 1596 or 1597, when *The Merchant of Venice* was probably written and first performed, William Shakespeare was an experienced man of the theatre and a famous and skilful writer. He had already written *Romeo and Juliet*, *A Midsummer Night's Dream* and *Richard III*, for example, and had published the long poems *Venus and Adonis* and *The Rape of Lucrece*, which brought him to the attention of possible wealthy patrons. On 22 July 1598 'a book of *The Merchant of Venice* or otherwise called *The Jew of Venice*' was entered in the Stationer's Register (an official list of all printed books), probably in an attempt by Shakespeare's acting company, The Lord Chamberlain's Men, to stop it from being printed by anyone else.

SOURCES

Just as with so many of his plays, Shakespeare took ideas from a lot of different places to make a new and fascinating story. There is a tale in a book called *Il Pecorone* by the Italian writer Ser Giovanni, which gave Shakespeare some basic ideas for his play.

Il Pecorone – which means 'the big sheep' or 'the fool' – was published in 1558. As it wasn't translated into English, Shakespeare quite possibly read it in Italian. But the idea of the three caskets, which Portia's suitors must choose between, doesn't come from this story. It appears in a lot of tales, and Shakespeare probably found it in Italian or English collections of stories such as Boccaccio's *Decameron* or John Gower's *Confessio Amantis*.

In writing a play about a Jew, Shakespeare was following a trend.

William Shakespeare, an oil painting, probably by John Taylor and dated 1610. It hangs in the National Portrait Gallery.

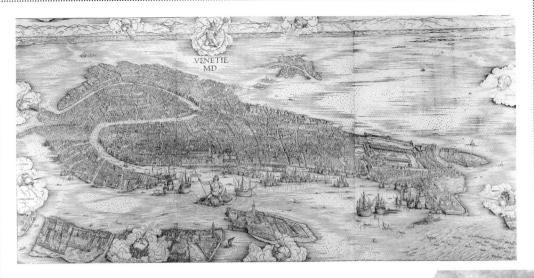

Part of a woodcut said to be by Jacopo de' Barbari, 1500, showing a bird's-eye view of Venice.

Christopher Marlowe had had a great success in 1589 with *The Jew of Malta*, and Shakespeare may well have got the idea of a Jewish girl marrying a Christian (as **Jessica** marries **Lorenzo**) from that play. There were other plays about Jews at this time too.

PREJUDICE

Most Londoners would never have seen a Jew. People in the once thriving Jewish community had been expelled as long ago as 1290, after many years of being forced to wear a yellow badge to mark them out. Prejudice grew out of ignorance. Although a few had returned, including a pocket of Portuguese Jews, on the whole they were seen as strange and different, and hated as the people held responsible for the death of Jesus.

Shakespeare's **Shylock** is a much more complex character than Marlowe's Jew, Barabas.

But some people believe the play is deeply anti-Semitic. They feel it is a play which should no longer be performed because it repeats and reinforces prejudices about Jews. Others see Shylock as a tragic figure, trapped by prejudice and driven to revenge by the treatment he gets.

The Merchant of Venice is one of Shakespeare's most disturbing creations. The playwright's insight into human nature never fails to surprise and puzzle his audience. The play is full of joy and energy but it is never far away from darkness and pain. It deals with serious matters, and yet can be wonderfully funny. Above all it asks questions about trust and tolerance which remain as fresh and as challenging now as when it was written.

THE CHARACTERS

Antonio is a merchant of Venice, who borrows money from Shylock to lend to his friend Bassanio.

Bassanio is Antonio's friend. He is courting Portia.

Leonardo is Bassanio's servant.

Lorenzo is a friend of Antonio and Bassanio. He elopes with Shylock's daughter, Jessica.

Graziano is also a friend of Antonio and Bassanio. He will marry Nerissa, Portia's maid.

Salerio and **Solanio** are friends of Antonio and Bassanio.

Shylock is a Jew of Venice, who lends money to Antonio.

Jessica is Shylock's daughter. She runs away to become a Christian and marry Lorenzo, taking Shylock's money and jewels with her.

Tubal is another Jew of Venice.

Launcelot Gobbo with his old father in a 1981 Royal Shakespeare Company (RSC) production at Stratford.

Shylock (Anthony Sher), Antonio (John Carlisle) and Bassanio (Nicholas Farrell) in Bill Alexander's production at Stratford, 1987.

Launcelot Gobbo is Shylock's servant. He later leaves Shylock and becomes Bassanio's servant.

Old Gobbo is Launcelot's father.

Portia is an heiress who lives at Belmont near Venice. Before he died, her father insisted she must only marry the man who chose of three caskets (one of gold, one of silver, one of lead) the one with her portrait in.

Nerissa is Portia's maid, who will marry Graziano.

Balthasar and **Stefano** are Portia's servants.

The Prince of Aragon and **The Prince of Morocco** come to Belmont wishing to marry Portia and try to solve the riddle of the caskets.

The Duke of Venice presides at the trial of Antonio.

There are also a **jailer**, **attendants**, **servants** and **magnificoes** (lords) **of Venice**.

WHAT HAPPENS
IN THE PLAY

Antonio, a merchant of Venice, is telling **Salerio** and **Solanio** that he is sad. They ask if he is anxious about the safety of his ships, due in to Venice at any time, but he denies it. They then ask if he's in love but Antonio dismisses the idea. **Bassanio**, **Lorenzo** and **Graziano** arrive and after Salerio and Solanio have gone, Graziano does his best to cheer up Antonio, but without success. Soon he and Lorenzo leave, arranging to meet them all again that evening.

Bassanio tells Antonio that he is in love with **Portia**, whose father has recently died. He is in despair as he hasn't the money to compete with the rich men who want to marry her. He asks Antonio for a loan – although he has borrowed a good deal from him already. Bassanio promises that if he marries Portia, Antonio will get back everything he has ever borrowed. But Antonio says that until his ships arrive safely he has no money to lend to Bassanio.

In Belmont, Portia and **Nerissa** are discussing the men who are coming to ask for Portia's hand in marriage. Portia only likes Bassanio. News comes that the **Princes of Morocco** and **Aragon** have arrived.

A MERRY BOND

Meanwhile, back in Venice, Bassanio has approached **Shylock** for a loan. Shylock agrees, but only if someone will repay the loan, with interest, if Bassanio cannot. Bassanio asks Antonio to meet Shylock and a deal is struck: if Bassanio is unable to repay, then Shylock will cut off a pound of Antonio's flesh. Shylock doesn't seem to be serious, calling it 'a merry bond', and in any case Antonio is full of confidence:

'In this there can be no dismay. My ships come home a month before the day.'

The Prince of Morocco arrives to woo Portia. She tells him the bargain: he must choose of three caskets (gold, silver and lead) the one which contains her portrait.

'Who chooseth me shall get as much as he deserves.' The Prince of Aragon decides on the silver casket in the RSC's 1984 production, directed by John Caird.

If he chooses the right one, he can marry her and share her wealth; if he makes the wrong choice, he must agree never to marry anyone. He accepts the deal.

Meanwhile in Venice, Shylock's servant **Launcelot Gobbo** is trying to decide whether to stay with the Jew or run away. He battles with his conscience and decides to leave. His old, blind father arrives. Launcelot asks for an introduction to Bassanio, whom he wants to serve instead of Shylock. Bassanio now joins them and agrees that Launcelot should become his servant. After the Gobbos have gone, Graziano appears and begs to be allowed to go with Bassanio to Belmont.

JESSICA RUNS AWAY

Launcelot Gobbo says farewell to Shylock's daughter, **Jessica**, who gives him a letter for Lorenzo. She is planning to run away, marry him and become a Christian. Lorenzo gets the letter and with his friends plans to take Jessica away that very night while Shylock is away from home.

That evening Shylock goes out, trusting Jessica to look after the house. Soon after, Lorenzo and his friends arrive, wearing masks as if for a party. Jessica goes with them, taking Shylock's money and jewels.

Once more the scene changes to Belmont where the Prince of Morocco has to make his choice between the caskets of gold, silver and lead. He chooses the gold casket – he's wrong, and a message inside reminds him:

'All that glisters is not gold.'

Later that night in Venice Shylock discovers his betrayal by Jessica, to the pleasure of Antonio's friends, while in Belmont another suitor arrives – the Prince of Aragon. He too makes his choice – silver – but he, too, is wrong. The Prince leaves, and a message comes for Portia that Bassanio has arrived.

DISASTER FOR ANTONIO

News arrives in Venice that one of Antonio's ships has been wrecked. His friends, Salerio and Solanio, are at the Rialto (where merchants met to make deals and obtain information about trade) when Shylock arrives. Hearing that Antonio has lost his fortune and will not be able to repay Bassanio's loan, Shylock decides to hold Antonio to his word, saying:

'Let him look to his bond.'

Salerio tries to laugh off the taking of a pound of flesh; but Shylock is out for revenge. He feels he has been insulted by Antonio, as by all the Christian merchants of Venice. To make things worse, they have taken Jessica away from him. He will have the flesh: 'If it will feed nothing else, it will feed my revenge.' All the pent-up sense of the wrong done to his people overflows:

'I am a Jew ... If you prick us do we not bleed? If you tickle us do we not laugh? If you poison us do we not die? And if you wrong us shall we not revenge?'

As Antonio's friends leave, another Jew, **Tubal**, arrives with the news that more of Antonio's ships have been sunk: he is ruined.

'What, what, what? ill luck, ill luck?' Shylock, played by Ian MacDiarmid, hears the news of the loss of Antonio's ships from Tubal.

BASSANIO'S CHOICE

Meanwhile in Belmont Bassanio is preparing to choose a casket. Although Portia is sure she loves him, she has sworn not to give away the secret. He must choose without any help from her. With much care he rejects the beautiful gold and silver caskets and picks the simple lead one. He is right. The portrait is inside with a message telling him to

'Turn you where your lady is, And claim her with a loving kiss.'

Antonio's friends arrive with Jessica and give the bad news about the merchant's losses. Portia tells Bassanio that he should go back to Venice. She will give him the money he needs to help Antonio.

In Venice Antonio is in prison. The merchant tries to renegotiate but Shylock refuses:

'I'll have no speaking. I will have my bond.'

Back in Belmont Portia has decided to help Bassanio: she will disguise herself as a lawyer and use her skill and knowledge to defend Antonio in court.

JUSTICE?

The day of the court hearing has arrived. The **Duke of Venice** tries to comfort Antonio, who is resigned to his fate. Shylock now comes into the court. The Duke invites him to work out a compromise, to show mercy:

'We all expect a gentle answer, Jew.'

Shylock, however, is firm. He argues that he must take his stand on the law. He repeats that a man's word is his bond. It is the duty of government and law to ensure that he pays what he owes. Bassanio offers to pay the money, and more. Shylock has lent three thousand ducats; he can have six thousand. But Shylock rejects it: not even for six times six thousand ducats will he compromise.

Portia arrives, dressed as Balthasar, a lawyer from Rome. She brings Shylock and Antonio forward. She accepts that Antonio has failed to meet the agreed terms.

She asks Shylock to show mercy. He refuses. He refuses to accept the money from Bassanio. Portia/Balthasar now seems to be on Shylock's side. To the fury of the court and Shylock's satisfaction, she gives him the right to the pound of flesh. Just as he has taken a knife to cut it off, she stops him. She points out that the bond speaks of flesh, but not blood. The law protects citizens of Venice from plots against their life. So Shylock cannot shed a drop of Antonio's blood – simply to consider doing so is punishable.

Shylock recognizes he is defeated by the very terms of strict justice on which, in his own anger, he had taken a stand. He tries to bargain, but all his offers are rejected. He leaves the court a beaten man: forced to agree that all his possessions will go to Jessica and Lorenzo, but worst of all, forced to become a Christian.

The trial of Antonio. Shylock (David Suchet) confronts Portia/Balthasar (Sinead Cusack) in the RSC production in 1981.

THE RING

After Shylock has gone, Bassanio thanks Portia/Balthasar and offers to give her a token of their gratitude. The lawyer asks Bassanio for a ring that Portia has given him. Reluctantly he hands it over. The lawyer takes the ring and leaves.

BELMONT

In Belmont, Jessica and Lorenzo are in the garden. It is night and they are enjoying its romantic beauty. They are disturbed, first by **Stefano**, Portia's servant, telling them his mistress will be back before dawn, and then by Launcelot Gobbo, who says that Bassanio, his master, will be coming in the morning.

When they are alone again, Lorenzo calls for music:

> **'With sweetest touches pierce
> your mistress' ear
> And draw her home with music.'**

Jessica and Lorenzo lie together, listening, bewitched by its sweetness and the starry night.

Portia and Nerissa arrive, quickly followed by Bassanio, Antonio and their friends. Graziano has fallen in love with Nerissa and has come to woo her.

The men, of course, have not guessed that Balthasar the lawyer was really Portia, and when she asks Bassanio about the ring, he lies, saying he has lost it. But Portia shows it to him, saying the lawyer gave it to her. And Nerissa says that she has been with the lawyer's clerk. Both Graziano and Bassanio are shocked: have the women been unfaithful?

TYING UP LOOSE ENDS

Portia now ties up all the loose ends. She admits that she and Nerissa were in Venice in disguise. She also tells Antonio that his ships have indeed arrived safely and he is still a rich man. Nerissa shows Shylock's agreement to Lorenzo and Jesssica – they will have his wealth.

All seems to end well enough, though the audience can hardly forget Shylock's pain and the shocks and surprises so many of the men have had. Antonio's light-heartedness about the deal with Shylock has brought him near to death. Bassanio's selfishness in wanting money has put his friend Antonio in danger, and Portia has shown how mean he can be, giving away the ring she has given him to keep.

'How sweet the moonlight sleeps upon this bank ...'
Lorenzo (Mark Lewis Jones) and Jessica (Kate Duchêne) enjoy the beauty of the night in the garden at Belmont, RSC, 1993

MERCHANTS
AND MONEYLENDERS

I n 1598 the play was described as '… *The Merchant of Venice* or otherwise called *The Jew of Venice*'. It was printed in 1600 as *The Comical History of the Merchant of Venice*. The various titles give an indication of the range of ideas in the play. Is the central character **Antonio**, the merchant, or **Shylock**, the Jew, who is a moneylender? Is it right to call the play a comedy? While some characters find love and happiness, others go off to loneliness and despair. Even those who do live 'happily ever after' have had painful experiences which make them sadder and wiser. Above all the play is about trade, making deals and taking chances, honesty and trust, and justice and mercy.

THE MERCHANTS AND THE JEWS OF VENICE

For hundreds of years the harbours of Venice on the east coast of Italy had been at the centre of trade between Europe and the Orient. Venetian merchants bought silks and spices (especially pepper), jewellery, fine pottery, silver, dyes and medicines from Turkey, the Middle East, and even China. They sold them at a great profit to the countries of northern Europe. Christian merchants like Antonio needed to borrow money to set up the trading expeditions that would make them rich.

Although the Jews of Europe were barred from many ways of earning a living, they were allowed to lend money for profit (called usury), and merchants turned to Jews when they needed loans. The moneylenders charged interest on the loan so merchants had to pay back more than they originally borrowed, but this would easily have been covered by the profits they made from their trade.

An illustration of a Venetian nobleman promising to keep the laws of Venice, from a book called *Giuramento of the Procurator Girolomo Zane*. The artist is unknown, but the picture is dated about 1570. It is illuminated on vellum.

Christians relied on Jews for a supply of money, but could Jews rely on Christians? Jews were tolerated as moneylenders but they were quickly blamed when things went wrong. They had little protection in law, and public opinion was against them. Does Shylock feel he must drive a hard bargain because he can't trust the merchant to keep the deal? And why does Antonio accept 'a pound of flesh' as the terms of the loan? Perhaps he so much wants to help **Bassanio**, is so sure of the return of his fleet of ships, and is so scornful of Shylock, that he doesn't take it seriously.

The play is about a Christian and a Jew, a merchant and a moneylender. Shakespeare shows us two men each of whom has something the other wants. Shylock has the money Antonio needs; Antonio has the respect and social standing that Shylock, as a Jew, cannot have.

THE MERCHANT OF STRATFORD

William Shakespeare's father, John, was a merchant in Stratford. Not only did he make high quality white leather goods, he also traded in other things – buying cheaply and selling at a profit. John Shakespeare was a moneylender as well, at a time when usury was still illegal, although essential for trading. In the early 1590s, John's fortunes declined and he was afraid of being arrested for debt. When Shakespeare wrote about trade and moneylending in *The Merchant of Venice,* he was exploring a world he knew from the inside, and was aware of its risks as well as its glamour.

Portia (Penny Downie) and Bassanio (Owen Teale) in David Thacker's production for the RSC, 1993.

'THEN MUST THE JEW BE MERCIFUL?'

When Antonio is unable to repay the money he has borrowed, Shylock takes him into a court of law for justice. The battle between Shylock and Balthasar (**Portia** in disguise) is often seen as a struggle between the Jewish concern for 'the letter of the law' and the Christian willingness to show mercy. This is too simple. When Shylock insists on justice and rejects any suggestion of compromise, he is taking his stand on a particular interpretation of the law – he had a deal with Antonio; Antonio has defaulted; the bond must be repaid. Shylock even tells the **Duke** that any compromise would ruin the reputation of Venice as a place in which to do business.

On a strict reading of the law, Shylock has a case, but Portia/Balthasar argues that if the law is seen only as a way of settling disputes between two individuals, then the strongest will win. Mercy is about compassion and compromise, but above all it is the right of a court to mitigate: that is, a court cannot overturn the law, but it can try to lessen its extreme effects. Mercy is as much a part of honest dealing as is the demand for the pound of flesh.

Shylock (played by Antony Sher) is cruelly baited by the Christians of Venice in Bill Alexander's 1987 RSC production.

SHYLOCK'S BETRAYAL

Why does Shylock insist on justice according to the letter of the law? Some productions of the play have insisted on the anti-Semitic interpretation that all Jews are wicked, and therefore Shylock is too. Others, accepting that this sort of generalization is wrong, and based on unthinking prejudice, have seen Shylock as a wicked man, who happens to be a Jew.

But some have looked more deeply. Shylock, as a Jew in a Christian city, has had to fight for survival. His experience has told him not to trust anyone. He says that Christian merchants insulted him even when they wanted to borrow money from him. And then his daughter **Jessica** betrays him, eloping with **Lorenzo**, a Christian. Maybe Shylock, hurt and angry at the loss of his daughter and the jewels she took with her, wants to get his own back.

VENICE AND BELMONT

Although much of the play is set in the bustling public world of Venice, it is contrasted with Belmont, Portia's home outside the city. This is a private, intimate place of love, joy and music. Lovers or would-be lovers come to Belmont; it could hardly be more different from Venice. And yet, Shakespeare overturns our certainties. Portia is beautiful, intelligent and witty.

By the terms of her late father's will, though, she must marry the man who makes the right choice in a test. She is like a piece of merchandise herself, waiting to be claimed.

Portia's suitors in Belmont, the **Princes of Morocco** and **Aragon**, have to take the sort of risk any merchant must, making unseen bids for goods, as they guess in which of the caskets Portia's portrait is to be found. Like inexperienced traders, they are conned by outside appearances, choosing the gold and silver boxes, learning to their cost that 'all that glisters is not gold …'

Bassanio chooses the lead casket because, like a clever merchant, he is prepared to take a calculated risk. Bassanio is successful and Portia gets the man she wants, but Shakespeare doesn't let the audience forget that in his time women were the property of their husbands, no matter how clever or rich they were.

And Portia is certainly clever. She can outsmart the Venetians in the law courts. She cynically traps Bassanio by getting him to give her the ring, showing how far he has still to go before he can be trusted. Only Shylock is a real match for her, but she backs him into a position where he must either die or lose everything. In the law court and in Belmont, too, Portia shows up the men as often selfish, arrogant and foolish.

THE MERCHANT OF VENICE
ON STAGE

We do not know exactly when or where *The Merchant of Venice* was first performed. It is mentioned by a law student called Francis Meres in his book *Palladis Tamia* in 1598. The printed version of 1600 says that it has been 'divers times [often] acted by the Lord Chamberlain's Servants'. The first recorded performance was on Sunday 10 February 1605 when King James I saw it performed. The King must have liked what he saw because he asked for another performance two days later.

It is likely that *The Merchant of Venice* was still performed after Shakespeare's death in 1616 but the next certain date is 1701, when a much rewritten version, called *The Jew of Venice*, was played at Drury Lane in London. **Shylock** was a figure of fun, played by the comic actor Thomas Doggett, and **Bassanio** became the central character. Much of Shakespeare's text was cut out or greatly changed.

CHARLES MACKLIN

The Jew of Venice was performed for forty years, until 14 February 1741.

On that day, the Irish actor Charles Macklin strode on to the stage at Drury Lane in a restored version of Shakespeare's play, 136 years almost to the day since its last known full performance. Macklin wiped away the memory of Shylock as a comic character. His performance so disturbed King George II that he suggested the whole House of Commons should be sent to see it to give them a fright.

Macklin's Shylock was a vicious villain out for revenge, growling out his lines, glaring at his enemies with eyes that were 'like a tiger peeping out of the bush', according to a fellow actor. He played Shylock for nearly fifty years until, just before his ninetieth birthday, his memory failed him during a performance, and he retired from the stage.

Edmund Kean as Shylock, a man of dignity even in defeat.

EDMUND KEAN

On 26 January 1814 a little known actor stood in the wings at Drury Lane waiting to go on stage as Shylock. Other actors shook their heads doubtfully. He wasn't wearing a dirty gown and a red wig – didn't he know this was how Shylock was supposed to appear? But Edmund Kean, making his first London appearance, had other ideas. If his Shylock was a villain, he would have humanity too, a man of dignity even in defeat. Playgoers were struck by the glare of contempt with which he fixed **Graziano** as he left the stage for the last time after the trial.

Kean's Shylock was proud to be a Jew. Maybe as a man who felt persecuted and misunderstood himself, Kean recognized Shylock's own struggle for survival among those who hated him.

HENRY IRVING

If Macklin rescued Shakespeare's revenging villain, and Kean rediscovered the human face of Shylock, Henry Irving, one of the greatest actors of the nineteenth century, presented a Jew in almost complete command of himself and his feelings. Although his control broke down when **Jessica** ran away, by the trial scene it was completely regained as he pursued his plan for revenge with ice-cold restraint.

One critic gives a picture of Irving's Shylock at the trial, listening 'with the horrible stillness and fascination of the rattlesnake'. Throughout, Irving wanted to show how Shylock was driven to revenge by the prejudice and hatred of those around him. This Jew was bearing the weight of the sorrows of all his people – the victim, exhausted by suffering.

Henry Irving as Shylock at the Lyceum Theatre, London, 1879.

DIRECTING
THE MERCHANT OF VENICE

Ever since Charles Macklin brought Shakespeare's text back on to the stage in 1741, *The Merchant of Venice* has remained a favourite with audiences. They have wanted to see great actors and actresses as **Shylock** and **Portia**, and the actors and actresses have wanted to show their skills in these demanding parts. In the eighteenth and nineteenth centuries the leading actor would make decisions about scenery, costumes and even the exits and entrances of other actors. In the twentieth century this job has increasingly been taken by the director, who guides the work of everyone else, bringing a sense of unity and meaning to a production.

Bassanio played by Owen Teale in the steel-framed set designed by Shelagh Keegan at the RSC, 1993.

TRAGEDY OR COMEDY?

As they work on a play, directors and actors have to ask questions about it, and the decisions they reach can make an enormous difference to what an audience will see and hear. One of the first things that has to be decided is whether it is a comedy or a tragedy. Shakespeare's own actors called it a comedy, but we don't know what their production looked like or how it came across to an audience. Many people think that the part of Shylock in Shakespeare's company was played by the great tragic actor Richard Burbage (who also played Hamlet, Othello and Macbeth), but some scholars have suggested it was in fact played by the comedian Will Kemp (who probably played Bottom in *A Midsummer Night's Dream*). What the Chamberlain's Men decided about casting (which actor played what part) would have made a real difference to the play.

In 1709 Nicholas Rowe prepared an edition of Shakespeare's plays. Writing about *The Merchant of Venice*, he said:

'*... we have seen ... the part of the Jew performed by an excellent comedian yet I ... think it was designed tragically by the author. There appears in it such a deadly spirit of revenge, such a savage fierceness ... and such ... cruelty and mischief, as cannot agree either with the style or characters of comedy.*'

Most actors and directors now agree.

DESIGNING THE PLAY

Directors and designers need to agree about the ideas in the play and how these can best be expressed visually. In the nineteenth century no expense would have been spared in creating scenery that showed Venice with its canals and bridges, and Belmont set in a beautiful garden. Gradually tastes have changed and designers increasingly began to 'suggest' Venice or Belmont – a bridge perhaps, or the three caskets of gold, silver and lead.

Theodore Komisarjevsky's set for a production in 1932. A critic said: 'He has fantasticalised *The Merchant of Venice* beyond all knowledge.'

Some directors and designers have looked for modern parallels. These have sometimes been vicious: in 1943 the Burgtheater in Vienna performed the play as a way of celebrating the destruction of the Jews by the Nazis. The Shylock of Werner Krauss was a brutal caricature played for the nastiest of laughs.

When David Thacker directed the play for the RSC in Stratford in 1993, he drew out the similarities between the commercial world of sixteenth-century Venice and the financial institutions of modern London. David Thacker and his designer Shelagh Keegan created a set of chrome and steel scaffolding. Characters wore designer suits and carried lap-tops. Everything was calculated to bring into focus the idea that money can drive people to do terrible things to one another.

THE TEXT OF THE PLAY

Directors and actors also have to make choices about the words they will speak. This might seem strange. Surely we all know what Shakespeare wrote? But nearly all the plays were printed in two early versions: Quartos, which appeared in Shakespeare's lifetime and the Folio, published in 1623, seven years after his death.

While the Folio texts were probably the versions that were regularly performed, the Quartos came from a range of sources. Some – the Quarto of *Hamlet* for instance – were probably based on actors' memories. Others, including the Quarto of *The Merchant of Venice* which was printed in 1600, were taken from working scripts, maybe even Shakespeare's own. There are many detailed differences between the texts in the Folio and the Quarto, and decisions have to be made about which to use.

Other choices about the text can be more controversial. When David Thacker was preparing the script for the 1993 production at Stratford, he decided to cut some lines to help the characters develop their roles more sympathetically. Shylock's line 'I hate him for he is a Christian' was taken out, as were Portia's lines about the **Prince of Morocco**, which seem racist today.

The title page from the first Quarto of
The Merchant of Venice, 1600.

On the other hand, when Bill Alexander directed the play at Stratford in 1987 with Antony Sher as Shylock, they wanted to drive home the anti-Semitic and racist attitudes of all the Christians, including Portia. So they left in her comments about the black Prince of Morocco which, as they were delivered to **Nerissa** who was played on this occasion by a black actress, were shocking in their unthinking racism.

Bill Alexander's production was remarkable for the viciousness of its Venetians. The upper-class yobs like **Solanio** and **Graziano** could accept Nerissa as honorary white and **Jessica** as honorary Christian, while laughing at Morocco and constantly spitting at Shylock.

The most excellent
Historie of the *Merchant of Venice*.

VVith the extreame crueltie of *Shylocke* the Iewe towards the sayd Merchant, in cutting a iust pound of his flesh: and the obtayning of *Portia* by the choyse of three chests.

As it hath beene diuers times acted by the Lord Chamberlaine his Seruants.

Written by William Shakespeare.

AT LONDON,
Printed by *I. R.* for Thomas Heyes,
and are to be sold in Paules Church-yard, at the signe of the Greene Dragon.
1600.

MUSIC AND *THE MERCHANT*

Music plays a key role in many of Shakespeare's plays and is particularly important in *The Merchant of Venice*. In Shakespeare's day music was seen as an expression of harmony, of things fitting together. Elizabethans believed that the planets themselves moved in harmony; music copied and expressed this cosmic good order. Music in a Shakespeare play is not there to fill in the gaps between scenes – beautiful music indicates peace and love.

Belmont is a place of music. When **Lorenzo** and Jessica are waiting for Portia to return from Venice, they call for music. As it is played, Lorenzo speaks of the night and the stars, and the heavenly music only angels hear:

**'There's not the smallest orb
which thou behold'st
But in his motion like an
angel sings ...'**

Within the play as a whole it is a moment of rest and calm after the trial, before Portia and the others come back to Belmont.

Directors need to be alert to the many musical clues. For example, in the same speech Lorenzo concludes that 'the man that hath no music in himself' cannot be trusted. Is he referring to Shylock? This idea was developed when David Calder played Shylock in the 1993 production at Stratford – we saw him at home listening to classical music on a hi-fi. The assumptions were overturned: this Jew could appreciate beauty.

Shylock (David Calder) at home with Jessica (Kate Duchêne), Stratford, 1993.

PLAYING SHYLOCK

For more than 250 years, **Shylock** has been a role against which many great actors have tested themselves. Some have shown him as an out-and-out villain; others, especially since Edmund Kean and Henry Irving took the role in the nineteenth century, have found in the Jew of Venice a complex figure, driven to revenge by insults and the loss of his daughter.

Directors, critics, actors and their audiences are constantly asking: what did Shakespeare intend? Did he think Shylock was a villain or a hero? Should he be played for laughs? What should we be most aware of – his difference from the other characters, his Jewishness perhaps; or his similarity to them, the feelings he shares, the world of trade of which they are all a part?

ANTONY SHER

One of the most villainous of recent Shylocks was that of Antony Sher in Bill Alexander's 1987 production for the RSC. At one level he seemed a caricature Jew, a man proclaiming his difference by what he wore and how he spoke. But Sher wanted the play to be 'a comment on second-class citizens everywhere', and if his Shylock behaved badly in his lust for revenge it was because he was driven to it by the much worse behaviour of his opponents. It was as if an outsider is forced to be different in order to survive.

Laurence Olivier playing Shylock in Jonathan Miller's production at the National Theatre in 1970.

Antony Sher as a flamboyant Shylock at Stratford in 1987.

LAURENCE OLIVIER

How to move from being an accepted part of the Venetian economy to being an outcast is always a crucial matter for an actor playing Shylock. Some, like Laurence Olivier in Jonathan Miller's 1970 production at the National Theatre, see Shylock as an outsider trying to get in. Olivier showed a man imitating, often with comic results, upper-class Christian behaviour but in the end discovering that they were bigots and frauds. This Shylock wanted desperately to be accepted and only turned on the Christians when he discovered how completely they rejected him.

PATRICK STEWART

When Patrick Stewart played Shylock in John Barton's 1978 RSC production, the actor and director came to the conclusion that Shylock is 'an outsider who happens to be a Jew'. They concentrated on his universality – the characteristics he might share with others. So this Shylock was an unlikeable man: he treated **Jessica** badly; he could be arrogant and unforgiving when he thought he was winning, but when losing would do anything to survive – even laughing along with **Graziano**'s jokes in the trial! Patrick Stewart's Shylock was a tragic figure, brought down by his own failings, who just happened to be a Jew.

DAVID SUCHET

John Barton directed the play again in 1980, at Stratford, and this time David Suchet, playing Shylock, explored what it meant to be an outsider *because* he is a Jew. For Suchet, the Jewish element was 'unavoidable and very important'. He also recognized that Shylock presents another challenge to an actor: he is on stage for only seven scenes and behaves very differently in each one. Many actors try to iron out these differences to get a consistent character, but David Suchet believed that it was important to be inconsistent – 'to play each scene for what it was'. This way you built up a much more complex picture of the character as each new piece of the jigsaw slotted into place.

DAVID CALDER

For David Calder as Shylock in David Thacker's 1993 production for the RSC, the play draws a picture of an intolerant society which the Jew challenges. Shylock knows that **Antonio** hates him but says, in effect, 'We can work together, do business together, and perhaps a friendship could grow.' Shylock puts himself on the line in the name of racial and cultural tolerance. It is only after Jessica leaves him that he comes to believe this is impossible. The tragedy is of a man whose attempts to build bridges are rejected by the society in which he lives until all he has left is revenge.

PLAYING PORTIA

There are three great challenges for any actress playing **Portia**. First of all, she has to live in two different worlds: beautiful Belmont and money-making Venice. Second, for much of the play she is a lively young woman, but in the trial scene she must pretend to be a sharp male lawyer. And third, she has to speak one of the most famous speeches in all the plays of Shakespeare: 'The quality of mercy …'

ELLEN TERRY

When Henry Irving played **Shylock** in the nineteenth century, the great actress Ellen Terry was Portia. A critic who saw her performance described it as

'gracious and graceful, handsome, witty, loving and wise … Portia to the life.'

Later in her life Ellen Terry spoke of Portia's famous speech as a moving and beautiful piece of poetry, but it is more than that. It comes at a crucial point in the trial scene where it first introduces the choice Shylock can make. He can go for full payment of the bond – his 'pound of flesh' – or compromise and show compassion. When Portia as the lawyer Balthasar praises the virtue of mercy, she is actually leading Shylock into a trap.

If he agrees with her, he loses face; if he disagrees and insists on repayment, she has a much greater shock ready for him – he can have Antonio's flesh, but not his blood.

Ellen Terry herself recognized this double-edged nature of the words. It is a magnificent and persuasive speech about a great human virtue. But Portia/Balthasar uses it to help the Christians trap Shylock and defeat him. Beauty is a bait, like jam to catch a fly. Throughout this interpretation, the idea was beginning to take hold that Portia was less morally perfect than we might think.

PEGGY ASHCROFT

When Peggy Ashcroft was first asked to play Portia in the 1930s, she was determined that she would approach the speech as 'a way of advancing the argument', not as a self-contained bit of poetry. A critic at the time commented that 'the speech arrived so suddenly I couldn't believe we'd got there'. Although the production as a whole (directed by John Gielgud) was criticized for its oddities, there is no doubt that Peggy Ashcroft's Portia, all 'innocence and humour', a young woman learning about love, has influenced many actresses who have approached the part since.

DEBORAH FINDLAY

If Ellen Terry noticed that Portia does not always behave as well as we might think a beautiful young woman should, then Deborah Findlay, in Bill Alexander's 1987 RSC production, was encouraged to explore these nastier parts of Portia to the full.

Venice here was a city full of racial hatred. Belmont was not a place of peace and beauty, but as one critic said, 'a place of creeping violence' and Portia on her home territory was vulgar – she had to be to control the loutish behaviour of **Bassanio**, **Graziano** and **Lorenzo**, but she seemed to get a kick out of it too. Her racist comments about the **Prince of Morocco** (so often cut) were left in. She seemed to hate Shylock quite as much as the men did. At least one critic was persuaded that this Portia was:

> *'... a stuck-up daddy's girl*
> *as nasty as she ought to be but*
> *so rarely is ...'*

Portia (Peggy Ashcroft) confronts Shylock (Michael Redgrave) in a 1953 production at Stratford.

PENNY DOWNIE

Deborah Findlay showed the unacceptable side of Portia. When Penny Downie began to prepare for the role in David Thacker's 1993 production, she and the director decided that Portia herself should embody 'the quality of mercy' and that Belmont should be as different as possible from Venice.

Penny Downie's picture of Belmont was as 'a spiritual place', 'a place of liberation and healing'. The racist comments were cut out of the text and Portia and **Nerissa** wore long flowing evening dresses which were a great contrast to the steel set and sharp suits of Venice.

Portia (Deborah Findlay) and Nerissa (Pippa Guard) at Belmont. Stratford, 1987.

FRIENDSHIP

AND FOOLING

Shakespeare's plays are full of friendships, deep relationships between two people who are often of the same sex, which give comfort and support, and often act as the springboard for change in characters' understanding of themselves. Rosalind and Celia, for example, in *As You Like It*, who run away together to the Forest of Arden; or Antonio in *Twelfth Night* risking death for his friend Sebastian in the midst of the confusions and madness of Illyria.

ANTONIO AND BASSANIO

Some interpretations of *The Merchant of Venice* have explored the complex friendship between **Bassanio** and **Antonio** in new and challenging ways. Is Bassanio pursuing **Portia** for her money? He's an extravagant man, who's borrowed from Antonio before. And what about Antonio? Why is he sad at the beginning of the play? Recent productions, especially Bill Alexander's at Stratford in 1987, have raised the possibility that Antonio is homosexual, frustrated in his love for Bassanio, and saddened by Bassanio's pursuit of Portia. He agrees to help Bassanio borrow from **Shylock** out of love, which is never returned.

LAUNCELOT GOBBO

The comic roles in Shakespeare's plays are of two main kinds: the clown and the fool. The fool tends to be sharp witted, a good singer with an important part to play in the way the plot develops – like Feste in *Twelfth Night* or the Fool in *King Lear*. Fools were like court jesters: entertainers who are allowed to speak the truth, however uncomfortable that might be. Clowns got their laughs by seeming less intelligent. They were often dressed as men from the country, outwitted by quick-thinking townsmen. The scenes in which these clowns appear are often simply opportunities for set-piece routines, like modern-day stand-up comics.

Christopher Luscombe as Launcelot Gobbo.
Stratford, 1993.

In many ways **Launcelot Gobbo** is a clown, not a fool. He has a long speech in which he wrestles with his conscience (should be leave Shylock or not?) which seems to be there not least to give an actor a comic routine. He has a scene with his father which appears to be little more than a chance for knock-about comedy, and maybe ad-libbing – making up lines on the spot, a hallmark of comedians throughout the centuries. (When Rob Edwards played Launcelot in 1981 he livened up his blind father's slow exit at one performance by telling him to 'Mind the canals'. The audience fell about laughing; the director was rather less pleased!)

Antonio (Clifford Rose) and Bassanio (Owen Teale) in the RSC production of 1993–94.

Christopher Luscombe, who played Launcelot at Stratford in 1993, discovered there is more to the part than mere clowning. Like a fool (such as Feste, or Touchstone in *As You Like It*), he gets drawn into the plot by acting as a go-between for **Lorenzo** and **Jessica**. His witty conversation with Jessica about becoming a Christian brings a new moral dimension to the play. For Luscombe, Launcelot Gobbo became a complex character: resentful of his father, fond of Jessica, jealous of Lorenzo. He was a clown, telling jokes, sharing his confusions with the audience; but he was a person too who went on an 'emotional journey ... from oppressed Venetian servant to salvation at Belmont'.

TODAY

In March 1996 in Konstanz, a town on the border of Germany and Switzerland, a group of young people – French and German speakers studying Shakespeare – performed in the English Bookshop extracts from several of the plays. Suddenly a young man pulled a skull cap from his pocket and put it on his head. He looked at the audience: 'Ich bin Jude,' he said. 'I am a Jew … If you tickle us do we not laugh? If you poison us do we not die?'

THE SHADOW OF ANTI-SEMITISM

Since 1945 all productions of *The Merchant of Venice* have had to face up to the horror of the murder of millions of Jews by the Nazis during the Second World War. Some people have thought that the play is so anti-Semitic that it should never again be performed.

Some have tried to show that it is much more sympathetic to **Shylock**, while others have explored the hatred of the Jews as a fact of European life which must be challenged and defeated within this very play. But no director, actor or member of an audience at *The Merchant of Venice* can now escape the long shadow of the Nazi concentration camps.

Of course many things happen in the play which are not directly connected to the question of Shylock's rejection, revenge and destruction. After all, Shakespeare's own company called it *The Merchant of Venice*, and it deals with questions of money and trade, trust and the law – all as vital in sixteenth-century London (or Venice or even Stratford, where Shakespeare's own father was a merchant!) as they are today.

'A pound of flesh': Shylock (David Calder) prepares to take what he is owed from Antonio (Clifford Rose). Stratford, 1993.

For David Thacker the situation went deeper. Shakespeare contrasts Venice, the place of money, the place where Shylock wants his 'pound of flesh', and Belmont, a place of 'generosity, compassion, love and kindness', as Thacker put it. His vision was that those qualities could spread to Venice, and even to the traders of Venice such as **Antonio** and **Bassanio**, making it a better place.

THE OUTSIDER

That was Shylock's vision too, in Thacker's production, but the Jew was trapped by intolerance and hatred until his hopes for co-existence – and even friendship – were changed into the one thought of revenge.

Wherever we look in the play, the uncomfortable questions about Shylock's treatment cannot be avoided. It always comes back to the Jew being the outsider. Even if, as Antony Sher played Shylock, he is flamboyant, shouting out loud his difference from the rest of the world, the question is raised: 'What made him like this?' Antony Sher's Shylock had a yellow Star of David sewn on to his gown. This production too had a prominent Star of David painted on the back wall like some Nazi graffiti. No one in the audience could forget the history which connected Shylock of Venice with the millions of Jews transported to camps, shot, burnt, poisoned:

'If you poison us, do we not die?'

What made the young man in Konstanz in 1996 want to play Shylock, want to speak that particular speech? The audience was aware first of how Shylock is no different from anyone else: Jew or Christian, all share a common humanity. But it became clear that if we make someone or some group second-class, then tolerance is twisted into hatred and friendship into revenge. Shylock shows just how hard tolerance can be.

'I am a Jew ...' David Calder's Shylock. Stratford, 1993.

INDEX